THE TOURING CARAVAN

Andrew Jenkinson

Published in Great Britain in 2014 by Shire Publications Ltd, PO Box 883, Oxford, OX1 9PL, UK.

PO Box 3985, New York, NY 10185-3985, USA.

E-mail: shire@shirebooks.co.uk   www.shirebooks.co.uk

A CIP catalogue record for this book is available from the British Library.

Shire Library no. 796.   ISBN-13: 978 0 74781 401 6
PDF e-book ISBN: 978 1 78442 019 2
ePub ISBN: 978 1 78442 018 5

Andrew Jenkinson has asserted his right under the Copyright, Designs and Patents Act, 1988, to be identified as the author of this book.

Designed by Tony Truscott Designs, Sussex, UK and typeset in Garamond Pro and Gill Sans.

Printed in China through Worldprint Ltd.

14 15 16 17 18   10 9 8 7 6 5 4 3 2 1

COVER IMAGE
Cover design and photography by Peter Ashley. Front cover: 1931 Winchester caravan, with grateful thanks to Rob Finney at Steve Finney Caravans, Mamble, Worcestershire. Back cover detail: Caravan Club badge, collection of Rob Finney.

TITLE PAGE IMAGE
Owners of a 1970s Astral Apollo make the most of its facilities.

CONTENTS PAGE IMAGE
The 1971 Sprite Musketeer, an export model. Sprite had dominated the entry-level market through the 1950s and 1960s, but by the mid-1970s sales began to slip.

ACKNOWLEDGEMENTS
All images are from the author's own collection, and are copyright Andrew Jenkinson.

Shire Publications is supporting the Woodland Trust, the UK's leading woodland conservation charity, by funding the dedication of trees.

CONTENTS

EARLY BEGINNINGS   4

EXPANSION AND INNOVATION:
THE 1930s   12

NEW IDEAS AND BOOMING SALES:
1940–60   24

FORWARD DESIGN AND LARGE
CONCERNS: 1960–80   34

A NEW ERA: THE 1980s TO THE PRESENT   52

FURTHER READING   63

PLACES TO VISIT   63

INDEX   64

EARLY BEGINNINGS

THE IDEA OF having mobile holiday accommodation in the form of a caravan came about in the nineteenth century, amongst members of the upper class who had a romantic vision of roaming the highways and byways of Britain and sampling life as a gypsy family might do (the phrase 'Gentleman Gypsy' comes from this era). The difference was that their caravans were looked after by servants, who would usually be accommodated in a nearby tent – the home comforts these rich caravanners enjoyed were far removed from the realities of gypsy life.

Of course no caravan sites as such were available: a stopover meant finding a patch of land and simply making camp! Often a farmer's field by a river was chosen and in payment eggs and milk would be purchased. This seemingly idyllic gypsy life inspired one man to write diaries of his travels – laying the foundations of the leisure touring caravan experience we know today. This pioneering caravanner was Dr Gordon Stables.

Stables designed his caravan and had it built for him by the Bristol Coach & Wagon Company in 1885. He named it 'The Wanderer', and it was later donated to the Caravan Club. As an ex-Navy man and writer of stories for boys, he wrote about his exploits in his 'Land Yacht' (connecting his travels by road with his seafaring days). His books were read with interest, and by the early 1900s the growing band of rich caravanners formed an exclusive club, which would bring like-minded people together. It was to

Opposite: Dr Gordon Stables' caravan, The Wanderer, its interior fitted out as a bachelor gentleman's flat. Stables wrote several books in his caravan about his caravanning adventures.

Horse-drawn caravans were popular until the First World War; this is a more primitive design with the kitchen being placed outside. This photo was taken c. 1907, at the time when the Caravan Club was founded by J. Harris Stone.

be simply named the Caravan Club and was formed by J. Harris Stone in 1907, and grew slowly.

This period of time saw the true beginnings of the combustion engine. Motoring was taking off – though it was expensive – and it wasn't long before some caravan users looked at putting a caravan body on the chassis of an early lorry or even car; this new idea was given the name 'motorised caravan', a name that would stick many years later. The future looked decidedly uncertain for the horse-drawn caravan, mainly because by 1914 many horses had been requisitioned for the First World War, to be used on the front lines.

Car design at this time, however, was improving fast in terms of reliability and affordability. This progress would inspire the likes of Frederick Alcock in 1914 to build a trailer caravan for his 1913 Lanchester car. Streamlined for that period, its design resembled the shape of the Sprite 14 some forty years later. Alcock didn't put it into production, building it entirely for his own use.

The car-pulled caravan did not evolve into a fully-fledged touring caravan until after the First World War;

it was after 1919 that several makers of caravans would become prominent. Winchester, Car Cruiser, Eccles and Raven were best known, with many obscure makers following in their wake. Names such as Red Rics, Ensor, Piggott, and Cliffe were some of the lesser-known early pioneers of caravan manufacture in the early 1920s.

Caravan production was a hand-built affair and construction and design harked back to the horse-drawn caravans. The Caravan Club at first refused to let these new motorised caravans and trailer caravans into the club. After the war, horse-drawn caravans were still used, but this would change as motor caravans and trailer caravans gained popularity.

Soon after Eccles, other small concerns began building car-pulled trailer caravans in the early 1920s, such as Cliffe, who built mainly to the customer's specification.

In 1914 the Riley's father-and-son team (confusingly they were both named Bill) built a primitive motorhome, on a 1909 Talbot chassis. The plan was to produce these on a commercial scale, but the war put an end to the venture. When Bill Riley Junior was de-mobbed he convinced his father that trailer caravans had a future – though his

The first commercially built touring caravan was designed and manufactured in 1919 by Eccles, a company at the forefront of motorhome design and manufacture.

father wasn't totally convinced. However, by 1919 the Eccles Transport Company (a run-down concern that the Rileys had purchased after the war) had produced a motor caravan and a touring caravan. Both were sold so the decision was made to go into serious production. But the Rileys would need to market the idea of holidaying with a car-pulled caravan. With prices of £95 or more for a caravan, caravanning would still be limited to the rich.

Marketing was left to Riley Junior who towed the Eccles using his Rover car to various parts of the UK promoting the idea. It was a hard and slow process, with some sales being made to companies to either sell or hire out the Eccles caravans at a couple of pounds a week. One such company, The Holiday Caravanning Co. in Oxford, found that those who hired a caravan usually bought one after experiencing a caravanning break. These primitive caravans came equipped with a paraffin stove, lighting and cooking utensils.

No insulation or proper chassis was fitted and the tow hitch consisted of a leather pin coupling on the first Eccles; with no component manufacturers, the sparsely designed chassis was manufactured by the caravan producer. However, Eccles would soon become the true pioneers of both the coachbuilt motor caravan and touring caravan, plus the collapsible caravan design. The company also built showman specials with ornate designs demonstrating their high-quality craftsmanship.

New manufacturers soon appeared emulating Eccles; they saw the potential Eccles had shown in marketing as well as design and manufacture. Wilkinson Cox, founder of Raven and inventor of the caravan 'screw' corner steady, produced his early models resembling horse-drawn

By the early 1920s Bertram Hutchings had turned to car-pulled caravans. Within a few years the Winchester name was used and known for its luxury and quality fittings.

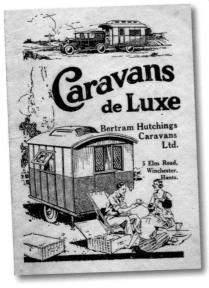

Caravans de Luxe

Bertram Hutchings Caravans Ltd.

5 Elm Road, Winchester, Hants.

designs (it wasn't until the mid-1930s that Ravens became more aerodynamic).

Bertram Hutchings began his caravan-building career after he and his wife had lived in a horse-drawn model after they were married. Soon he designed and built his own caravan and before long he entered the caravan business. Like most of the early manufacturers Hutchings went over to trailer caravans but had been operating a fleet of horse-drawn caravans, which he branded Winchester, named after the town where the works were based.

Caravan-building couple Arthur and Joy Gardener were to begin building a range of touring caravans named Summerfield. Later re-named Cheltenham by the 1930s, the firm prospered. As with most early caravans of the 1920s, the early Summerfields were box-like in design, basic but light considering the heavy materials. Early caravan designs were influenced by popular cars of the period such as Austin Sevens, Jowetts, Rovers and Morris Minors. In those days most caravan manufacturers used the Molly Croft roof design, better known as the 'lantern' roof – which had a raised section in the middle with small opening windows. This design was heavy, complex and more expensive to produce, so was usually fitted

Hutchings' first venture into caravans began with this horse-drawn caravan; within a few years Hutchings had a small fleet available for hire.

to deluxe models, but it offered more headroom and improved ventilation.

Another notable maker of this period was Piggott, who in five years of production created some interesting designs from just 3-metre body lengths. They used ideas such as bay windows that could be folded away for towing, opening out again once sited. Piggott also produced caravans with rear verandas and patented a construction method used in aircraft manufacture at the time.

Melvin Hart was another early pioneer of the touring caravan, though motorhomes was his main business. However Flatvan, Hart's company brand name, built super luxury motorhomes sometimes complete with a Flatvan trailer caravan on tow! Hart sold his caravans to the super rich, including to maharajahs, who demanded lavish interiors and only the best in quality and materials.

The Scottish firm Thomson, who were joiners, entered small-scale caravan manufacture in 1922 after building a few motor caravans. Very similar in design to Eccles caravans of that period Thomson would by the late 1920s move towards more streamlined designs. Many years later Thomson became a larger concern and well known in caravanning circles. Angela was another new 1920s maker, basing their models on the Eccles look. (The company was named after the founder's daughter Angela!)

Eccles had built collapsible caravans for a short time, but other makers such as Shadow from Coventry proved a greater success with their 1925 collapsible design. Trailavan in Birmingham had a folding caravan with solid sides and a solid roof that extended upwards. Once pitched, canvas was used to make up the top half of the caravan. Rice trailers used the same principle, becoming better known from 1925. Rice owners boasted of long continental trips with their Yorkshire-built folders, a fact that the makers were only too keen to use as PR.

Charles Ensor in the 1920s had fold-out kitchen extensions and toilet compartments in his caravan designs; such was the imagination used by those early makers. By the end of the 1920s caravanning had grown in popularity. Eccles was clearly ahead of the rest of the field with its modern production plant. Many new manufacturers would, like Eccles, operate small hire fleets to encourage buying customers. With car ownership rising and the middle classes also now being able to afford cars, caravanning would reach new heights.

Rare colour photograph of a 1920s Eccles Deluxe in the Devon countryside. Posed to show how good caravanning was for mind, body and soul, it was marketed as a way to forget everyday worries!

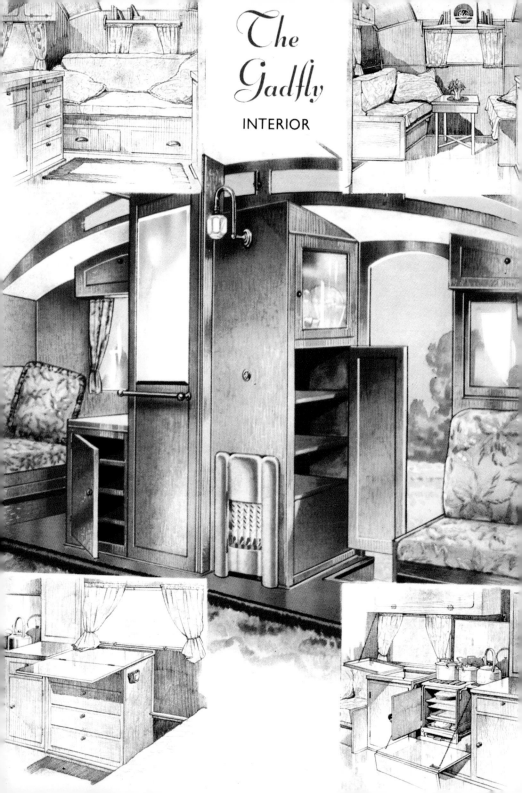

The Gadfly

INTERIOR

EXPANSION AND INNOVATION: THE 1930s

B Y THE 1930s caravanning was seen as an ideal form of holidaying and its popularity was much greater than it had been in the 1920s. The public would be further exposed to caravanning via several caravan-related events, including the 1932 rally organised by the publication *Autocar* at Minehead; this attracted over ninety caravans with several caravan manufacturers themselves attending. The rally garnered a great deal of attention and the following year another major rally was held at Cheltenham, expanding on the success of the Minehead event.

Various clubs, such as the Junior Car Club in 1932, had formed their own caravan sections. Attracting over three hundred new members by 1935, The Caravan Club was reformed and absorbed the Junior Car Club's caravan members. Owners' clubs were formed by some manufacturers, Eccles being the first. These clubs gave manufacturers brand loyalty, which would serve them well with customer feedback. They could then improve their models on users' experiences. New designs were sometimes implemented as a result of members' suggestions.

It was in this period that two caravan journals were launched. Although *Autocar* published a section on caravans it was clear a dedicated magazine was now needed. In May 1933, the first issue of *The Caravan & Trailer* magazine was launched, priced 6d and edited by F. L. M. Harris, who was also the owner. With a print run of six thousand copies each month it proved a success. Caravanning was now truly

Opposite:
Jubilee Caravans, based in Shrewsbury, had a strong customer base by 1939. This colour illustration shows their Gadfly four-berth model.

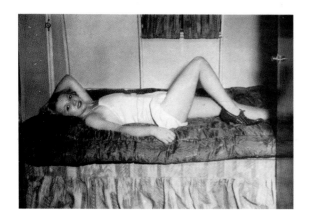

Manufacturers had famous personalities pose in their caravans. Eccles used Gracie Fields, while Northampton Caravans had this daring shot taken in 1938 of variety performer Vera McCarthy posing on the bed of their £119 Glider caravan.

recognised as a growing holiday activity. Several celebrities of the day (Gracie Fields and Nora Swinburne, for example) went caravanning and manufacturers were always keen to have a posing star photographed in one of their caravans. The Caravan Press, though small, would also play a great part in bringing manufacturers and dealers closer. Other progress in caravans came when the boss of Eccles, Bill Riley, fought hard to raise the permitted towing speed from 20 mph to 30 mph, which eventually came into force in April 1931.

In the 1930s gas entered the world of caravanning with paraffin-fuelled oil lamps and cookers becoming obsolete. By 1938 Botto gas had been replaced by the brand Calor with a new small cylinder design that was easy to store and handle and was available from over five hundred service depots in the UK.

In May 1939 another milestone in the caravan industry was reached with the founding of the trade organisation The National Caravan Council, which would give the industry a voice. The Council was set up to represent the industry in all areas, as it still does today.

Some early, small-scale firms faltered due to more intense competition, while the established brands such as Eccles, Winchester, Raven, Car Cruiser, Carlight and Cheltenham gained a bigger market share. Imported caravans were rare; some early imports such as the Covered Wagon from the United States were sold by the dealership Nomad Caravans in Surrey with little success.

Eccles was still leading the way into the new decade, producing its motor caravans alongside their touring models. The squarer original design had given way to more streamlined models by the early part of the 1930s. Most caravan design was driven by aerodynamics, influenced to some extent by car designs of this period. Eccles was pushing ahead with its manufacturing process in this decade.

The company had moved to new premises, which were enlarged in 1936 to keep up with ever-increasing demand. Using pre-fabricated furniture and having virtually all components built in-house the Eccles factory was prolific and highly efficient.

Eccles boasted in 1937 that they were the largest manufacturer of caravans on a global scale, with exports playing a major role. Eccles had been the first to export caravans in the early 1920s, seeing this area of the business growing; models were sold in France, Germany and Holland too. However, in Europe, caravan manufacturers were beginning to become established, and these would soon supply the growing home markets.

Interestingly, Eccles export models were basically the same as the UK versions but with some slight differences in the detail. For instance, the internal framework would

Although caravans in the 1930s were still hand built, Eccles was adopting quicker production techniques. The factory, shown here, was well organised and had all the latest machinery of the day installed.

CARAVANNING
en 1936

plus agréable que jamais
avec les Caravanes Anglaises légères

signées   ECCLES

be treated with anti-insect compound, and fly screens, on-board water tanks, increased ground clearance, heavy-duty axles and chassis, and a spare wheel/tyre were other additions on export models. Europe and tropical countries, in the Rileys' experience, proved that

By 1936 Eccles were leaders in the export market, selling caravans into France in large numbers.

The Eccles was tested under extreme conditions, with the Humber tow car shown here at an oasis in the Sahara in 1932. The trip was excellent for Eccles and caravanning in general, receiving good press coverage.

rough terrain needed an upgrade in specification. Eccles would test their caravans in other countries over poor terrain, proving their durability. The British-designed and -built caravans combined innovation with high quality, and in the view of continental buyers were among the best looking.

Eccles had developed its tourers to suit traditional and modern tastes. Streamlining would strongly feature in Eccles design but traditional lantern-roof models were produced with the emphasis being on luxury fittings. Models such as the Senator, President, and Coronation and (by 1939) the National, became well known. Eccles had also developed the 'lean-to tent' or awning, an accessory that keen enthusiasts used increasingly.

By 1938 Cheltenham had become another well-known caravan manufacturer, moving into the luxury end of the touring caravan market.

Cheltenham Caravans had slowly turned to more aerodynamic profiles by the early 1930s, building a strong following, and was one of many other companies operating in the Cheltenham area. Cheltenhams were designed to be lightweight and towable by smaller cars of the time. Customers could even choose the exterior colour to suit their towing vehicle if desired.

Car Cruiser had developed curved aerodynamic designs from 1930; the weight was also kept low. They were designed by Major Fleming Williams (or 'Streamline Bill', as he became known), a gifted artist, who used his talents to great effect in illustrating PR material for his company. Car Cruiser had moved to a new factory in Thames Ditton, which operated on several

Two Remarkable Models

The Cheltenham "Gazelle" Three Berth

The GAZELLE

Here is a Trailer which will "sell like hot cakes." Measuring 11 ft. 3 ins., this completely equipped model represents the finest value ever offered. A roomy, well-appointed and attractive caravan which can be towed by an 8 h.p. car.

Colour Scheme to Order. PRICE **£110**

The Cheltenham "Reindeer" Four Berth

The REINDEER

This model has been developed from the very successful 47C model of last year. It measures 13 ft. 6 ins. by 6 ft. 4 ins., and although a very light van it will appeal to the most fastidious. It can be easily towed by an 8 h.p. car. Fitted with standard Cheltenham refinements, this new "Reindeer" model is amazing value.

PRICE including full equipment **£115**

Colour Scheme to Order.

Car Cruisers of the early 1930s were distinctive and aerodynamic with Art Deco influencing their styling. Some users found the rear end of the van rather gloomy, due to the small rear windows.

different floors – although it was an improvement on the smaller and older original works, production wasn't as smooth as Eccles's, with parts having to be transported upstairs. Car Cruisers were priced around the £300 mark along with most of the competition in this market sector.

Raven, who had been manufacturing its very square-looking touring caravans up to the early 1930s, went over to the new streamlined look. Raven model names such as Dominion, Argosy and Argonette, and for 1937 the Wizard

Raven was another early caravan manufacturer who had built up success through the 1920s. By the 1930s Raven was producing more aerodynamic designs, such as this 1937 Wizard four-berth model.

(3.5 metres in length, a compact four-berth model) would be familiar to caravanners in this period.

Winchester had by 1930 become influenced by aerodynamics, moving to streamlined profiles for their models. Combining luxury with craftsmanship, the Winchester name became known for its detailed design with items such as hot water, baths,

showers, built-in radio and electric lighting. Winchester would be considered the Rolls Royce of the caravan world with only the well-to-do able to afford one.

Siddall, a new maker, produced crafted models with some unusual exteriors. The Family Four unusually had twin access doors, both mounted on the same side. Siddall would become known in the 1950s for luxury quality caravans, with names such as Hunter's Moon and Torbay being aspired to by keen clubmen. Neville Siddall had founded the company in 1932 having gained experience with Cheltenham Caravans.

There were now several small chassis suppliers for touring caravan manufacturers, although makes such

Interior of the Raven Wizard, showing its compact yet well-designed layout. The 1937 Wizard was single wall panelled.

Siddall Caravans produced up-market tourers such as this unusual twin-door Family Four model in 1939.

as Cheltenham Caravans continued to design and manufacture their own.

It is important to note at this point that caravan construction had been progressing alongside developments in design: in the late 1920s plywood sides had been used with a waterproof fabric covering them; internal ash-framed bodies, with an air gap between the exterior and interior panels, were commonly used in caravan construction in the 1930s. Pressed fibreboard was used by most manufacturers for the exterior panelling, with around five coats of full lead paint (adding considerable weight) for weather protection!

Canvas was used on the roof, and it was an annual job to give the roof a fresh coat of paint for winter. Many caravans from this era tended to leak, and rot could set in quickly, so painting was crucial. Insulation would be used in more expensive tourers and consisted of foil, latex, cork and glass fibre wool with cork under the floor.

By the 1930s the pin coupling had given way to the more dependable ball-type design, which gave a more stable tow.

The ball lock-on coupling had now replaced the unreliable pin unit from the previous decade, adding improved towing stability. Back then, towing most caravans above 25 mph usually caused a snaking effect. With leaf suspension employed, caravans tended to bounce around on rough roads due to the lack of shock absorbers.

Design improvements of this decade saw the addition of a screw hand-operated jockey wheel fixed by the caravan's coupling, making hitching up and manhandling the caravan easier. Interior toilet compartments in this period were gaining popularity after some years of resistance by users (toilet tents were used by caravanners who believed interior toilet compartments to pose a health hazard). Some makers fitted an exterior door for access to the toilet compartment, but by the end of the decade toilet compartments in tourers were quite a common feature.

With mass-produced components now becoming available to caravan manufacturers, the cost of caravans was driven down, making them more affordable than before. This encouraged new makers to come into the world of caravan manufacture. Names such as Glider, Jubilee, Bampton, Atlas, Carlight, Silver Ball, Burlingham, Adams, Cotswold, Airlite, Condor, Romany, Sunray, Wanderlust, Roleas, Rollalong, Rivers, Sandling, Fleetwing, Landover, Ace, Bristol, Dawn, Davan, Lolode, Luxonic, Pelham, Roundbay and Coventry Steel were all part of the expanding caravan-manufacturing industry.

Dealerships were also witnessing growth: Harrington's, Yorkshire Caravans, Roundstone, Cara-Cars, Perthshire Caravans, and MG Caravans were all selling and (in most cases) hiring out caravans for a growing caravanning public. Most of these dealers sold many of the popular makes of tourers. Dealers often became established from selling a single caravan, then a business from this one sale often quickly flourished.

With new manufacturers being founded almost on a monthly basis, the 1930s witnessed a number of new ideas – some were not to lead to commercial success, while others led the way for future caravan manufacturers. An influential figure in design and innovation was Clifford Dawtrey. Legend has it that he designed the first non-leaking car sunroof! Having worked for Jaguar cars, by the mid-1930s he had moved into caravan manufacture. His new company based in Coventry, Airlite Caravans, produced streamlined, lightweight and stylish tourers for just £100.

In Art Deco style with sweeping mouldings and leaded windows plus a lantern roof, the Airlite looked stylish back

The 1936 "Airlite" FOUR BERTH De Luxe
AT THE REVOLUTIONARY LOW PRICE OF 100 Gns. (EX WORKS)
EASY PAYMENT TERMS ARRANGED TO SUIT CUSTOMERS' REQUIREMENTS

Clifford Dawtrey founded his Airlite Company in the mid-1930s and his talent for design and ideas showed in his caravans. By 1937 he was using plastics for the exterior mouldings.

in 1936, then in its second year of production. Interior design saw a wardrobe on the entrance door, a loose table that folded down (like a modern caravan table design today), and wrap-around seating in the dinette area.

The following year, Dawtrey made his Airlites look more aerodynamic, using Bakelite, an early plastic material, which was applied to the caravan's corner edges. The production workers had to heat the material with an iron, then curve it around the edges. Although this gave the Airlites a smarter and more aerodynamic appearance it was costly and labour-intensive and proved to be part of Dawtrey's downfall. Some faults did occur in the process, causing water to enter the corners if application was hurried.

By the end of 1937 the company had shut down; Dawtrey wasn't to be defeated, however. By mid-1938 he had formed a new manufacturing company, Coventry Steel Caravans. His Silver Knight model was ash framed with a steel body, covered in felt then leathercloth, which increased the caravan's insulation. His luxury version, the Phantom Knight, was a classic design in every sense of the word. Steel bodied with porthole-influenced window design and complete with a rear chrome bumper, the Phantom looked superb. It was heavy and expensive, and with the Second World War looming, production was to be short-lived.

Making cheaper caravans meant low quality in most cases. However, Ace Caravans was able to sell its family model for less than £100 in 1938, thanks to its straightforward square design. Ace could mass-produce to a certain extent, helping to keep costs down, and had the

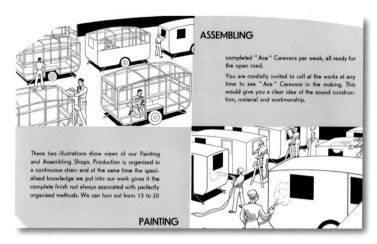

ASSEMBLING

completed "Ace" Caravans per week, all ready for the open road.

You are cordially invited to call at the works at any time to see "Ace" Caravans in the making. This would give you a clear idea of the sound construction, material and workmanship.

These two illustrations show views of our Painting and Assembling Shops. Production is organised in a continuous chain and at the same time the specialised knowledge we put into our work gives it the complete finish not always associated with perfectly organised methods. We can turn out from 15 to 20

PAINTING

Ace claimed to produce fifteen to twenty caravans a week in 1937 using a production plant not unlike Eccles with sectioned areas of the factory split up for various assembly jobs.

advantage of a well-organised factory and workforce. These were the top-selling caravans of that time, although after 1939 Ace disappeared.

With the decade coming to a close and with the outbreak of war in September 1939, caravan production would be hard hit. Shortage of materials and labour plus fuel rationing meant car owners had limited usage. But by this point the caravan-manufacturing industry had begun to establish itself in the UK, and was to expand further in forthcoming years.

Dawtrey's Airlite Company had folded by the end of 1937, but he came back with Coventry Steel Caravans. This is the Phantom Knight, built using all steel-bodied construction. It proved expensive to build, and was also heavy.

NEW IDEAS AND BOOMING SALES: 1940–60

WITH THE SECOND World War came petrol rationing and cars were forced off the road to be stored; caravans, similarly, were all of a sudden being placed on a site and left, becoming 'static caravans'. Owners began living in them, or used them just occasionally, classing them as living vans or holiday caravans. By 1940 The Caravan Club had over 1,600 members, a number that would increase significantly in subsequent years, but with most skilled labour taken for war work not many caravan makers would re-emerge after 1945.

The companies that survived the war did so mainly thanks to government contract work, which kept the factories open. Riley at Eccles had put in plans for mobile offices to the MOD as early as 1936, thus assuring a contract. Dawtrey had been thinking ahead too: his designs for trailer ambulances added corner steadies, four electric lights, an oil heater and a gravity-fed water tank. Thomson, who had been quietly producing some streamlined designs before the war, had also become involved in war work, as had Raven and Car Cruiser.

Caravans in the early 1940s were in short supply and those who had become homeless through heavy city bombing were desperate to have a roof over their heads. Prices became inflated and some poor examples were sold which had been shoddily built or maintained. With a shortage of materials, poor-quality caravans were not uncommon.

Opposite:
By the end of the 1950s the Sprite caravan was a market leader, and new models were launched. Pictured is the 1958 Alpine; a family model costing just £290, it became a bestseller for many years.

Positives did surface, however: after the war changes were afoot with new names, new production techniques and an even higher demand for caravans. New gluing methods and faster production meant caravans would become cheaper to build than before the war, passing the saving to customers.

The Eccles factory pioneered new flow-line production techniques. For 1945–6 they turned to producing a cheaper, simpler design named the Enterprise. Using jigs and new machines for cutting accurate sections of wood and building pre-formed panels, the assembly was speedy and accurate but also cost-effective, keeping the Enterprise affordable. Concentrating on one model meant that production was simple. Orders were quickly taken with buyers such as the US Air Force ordering them for the Burton Wood air base for living accommodation. In just over eighteen months, five hundred Enterprises had been sold, proving mass production was the way forward with simple designs for the mass market.

The rationing of materials in the post-war years made life hard for many; nevertheless, new makers such as Paladin, Berkeley, Willerby, Safari, Pemberton, Bluebird, Bailey and Streamlite were all active by the end of the 1940s, though some of these concerns had dabbled in caravans before the war.

One post-war manufacturer became particularly successful. Bill Knott had manufactured caravans in the late 1930s under the name Midland. Cheaply built, Knott sold them direct from his father's auction rooms in Poole, Dorset. After the war Knott went back into caravans but in a bigger way, branding them Bluebird Caravans. Knott

Eccles launched its £553 Enterprise in 1946, mass-producing it with methods learnt in war work where quantity and quality were key. Simple design inside and out made the Enterprise a success for Eccles.

looked at covering the whole market sector, from tourers to holiday static caravans plus permanent living caravans, and by the late 1950s he had launched the Bluebird Highwayman coachbuilt motorhome. Knott also built trailer horseboxes at his Poole works.

Bluebird's vast range of caravans was ever changing; problems with quality in the early days were ironed out by the late 1950s. Bluebird sales were booming, and model names such as Thunderbolt, Pathfinder, Forget-me-knot, Rambler, Sun Parlour and Sabrina became well known in caravanning circles.

The Parkstone factory was in full production, exporting Bluebirds in great numbers. Knott featured in a short Pathé newsreel film in 1959, showing how Knott had become a successful businessman.

Established in 1947, the small manufacturer Safari Caravans in Gloucester made several models including the tiny Minor, with its entrance door unusually placed over the front drawbar. Family models such as the Safari Four proved good sellers for the firm

Eccles PR photo making out the car was towing four new Eccles Enterpprise models!

The Pathfinder was just one of the many models Bluebird produced. By 1959 it was reported that Bluebird was turning out 350 caravans a week!

THE *New* BLUEBIRD PATHFINDER
THE HOLIDAY CARAVAN WITH STYLE!

Safari Caravans was established in 1948 and by the early 1950s offered models such as this Safari Four (from 1954).

and Safari became a well-respected luxury make in later years. Another post-war company, Bessacarr, would by the late 1950s become a luxury manufacturer and into the 1960s become a sought-after clubman make.

One of the most famous names in caravanning, Sprite, was produced by Alperson Products, established in 1947 by brothers Sam and Henry Alper. Materials were short but they produced their Streamlite Rover and the smaller Elf using ex-war surplus stock. A plastic board was used for the exterior, and the independent suspension system used was designed and built by Alpers. At over £600 though, the Streamlites proved costly and they were heavy. Sam Alper conducted some dealer research, to discover that they required

In late 1947 postwar manufacturer Alperson produced the Streamlite Rover and smaller Elf (pictured). These were replaced in 1949 by the Sprite caravan, costing £199.

affordable touring caravans that would prove durable and yet remain lightweight.

The Sprite itself was created in 1949, and went on sale for £199. It was lightweight, but would-be dealers needed convincing of its durability, so Alper set out to prove the Sprite's build quality, conducting several endurance tests (just as Eccles and Car Cruiser had done in the 1930s). Sam Alper entered a race on the Continent in 1952 covering over 10,000 miles in thirty-four days with his Sprite. The caravan remained intact, and Alper won the race, gaining export orders in the process. Sprite was a hit, and by the late 1950s Alperson had become a leading manufacturer.

Caravan manufacturers found the new boom in consumer spending by the mid-1950s a time of increased sales. George Holder founded the Paladin Trailavan Company in post-war Britain in 1947 having been involved with caravans in the late 1930s. At £1,236 the first design was a living caravan with slotted side walls for construction and insulated with Isoflex.

In 1949 he launched his £395 streamlined, lightweight, 4.26m family model, the Wisdom. This new tourer was to lead on to other models such as the Rapier, Pacemaker and Buccaneer.

Berkeley Caravans, founded by Charles Panter in the late 1940s, became another major manufacturer in the 1950s. Panter, like Dawtrey, was not afraid to put his own ideas into caravan design. In the Messenger, for example, the rear end panel folded down like a sun deck. Extending caravans, slide-out designs and the Europa (a steel-bodied tourer) all came out of the Berkeley factory. Panter used glass-reinforced plastic (GRP), a new material, in his Berkeley Delight in 1955.

The Wisdom was launched in 1949 and ran for several seasons using different profiles; this 1949/50 version was popular amongst families as it was easy and light to tow.

PALADIN 'WISDOM'

PRICE
£325
EX WORKS

Berkeley Coachwork produced interesting designs in the 1950s. Berkeley was another post-war manufacturer with experience in war work. The 1955 Courier pictured here sold well for the company at £485. Berkeley's portfolio included sports car manufacture.

Berkeley's sports car division used GRP shells but a lost US export order would eventually bring the company crashing down in 1959. Panter started up the caravan business again only to fail in 1961.

Willerby Caravans, established in 1948, built very crude tourers named Yorks, growing speedily with the boom in caravanning. By 1956 the factory in Willerby, on the outskirts of Hull, had entered into GRP construction with two models – the Vogue and Vista – but sales were limited due to their high price and weight. Willerby then pulled out of using GRP shell construction, and the more conventionally built Vagabond and Universal would be its mainstay of tourers. After acquiring Beverley-based Robin caravans in the early 1960s Willerby pulled out of touring caravans altogether, concentrating on static holiday caravans, using the Robin name in the tourer market.

Luxury caravans built by Siddall and Freeman did use GRP with great success in this era. Their clients were caravanners who could afford the best in touring caravans, and the price tag didn't put them off.

Cheltenham Caravans from 1956 would introduce GRP mouldings to create its classic profile for the roof and ends, leaving side exteriors finished in aluminium. Cheltenham was a clear leader for several years, mastering the technique of GRP construction without adding weight and too much cost.

Willerby had made vast improvements in design and quality by the end of the 1950s. The 1957 Universal was a typical touring family caravan from their range.

By the end of the 1950s most caravans were insulated and had aluminium (taking over from hardboard) exterior panels, but exterior design hadn't moved on much since the 1930s. Gas provided heat, cooking and lighting while chassis manufacturers such as B&B Trailers, Bowden and Peak Trailers grew in size with climbing caravan sales. Eccles, though, had lost out in market share even though it had launched successful new models such as the Alert and Coronation.

Glass fibre reinforced plastic (GRP), as a new material, was difficult to use in the caravan industry, but Cheltenham Caravans had most success. The Cheltenham Springbok from 1956 was the first Cheltenham model to use GRP panels in its construction.

Bailey was another post-war manufacturer. Established in 1947 with one model, by 1951 it had extended its range, the Maestro being their mainstay model running for many years.

Without question the finest value in holiday caravans to-day.

and the MAESTRO

The MAESTRO offers holidays happier than any you've had before. Easily towed behind a small car, the MAESTRO is strongly-built with all-steel chassis and aluminium exterior. Fully furnished, it has two single and one double bed, ample locker space and up-to-the-minute cooking unit. Believe it or not—its price is only ████ £325. Hard Board
£340 Aluminium Sides

Bristol-based Bailey, a new maker from 1948, had developed a range from just one model, which founder Martin Bailey had built and sold as a virtual one-off. Named Maestro, Bailey's tourer with its aluminium sides represented a quality caravan for the price (£340).

At this time, sites were growing in size and providing better facilities, which helped to drive an increase in sales of tourers. The city of Hull and its surrounding towns and villages became the nucleus of caravan manufacturing, with makes such as Astral, Cresta, Robin, Lissett, Welton and Sunbeam joining Willerby.

The caravan boom led to an increasing demand for cars with towing brackets. In 1952 the engineering firm C. P. Witter, based in Chester, designed and manufactured standard-fit towbars and worked alongside car manufacturers to create safer brackets that were easier to fit. The British Caravan Road Rally, first held in 1954, put caravans through their paces and proved an ideal way of testing towing stability and durability, and Witter was heavily involved.

The 1950s witnessed two amphibian caravan designs, the Duck by Raven, and the Otter, but sales were limited. Double-decker caravans also met with little success: in 1952 Peak Caravans launched its Diplomat, a twin-axled double-decker design, and Berkeley followed with the Statesman, but neither proved popular. Coventry Steel also dabbled in this sector, but the idea just didn't sell.

Dawtrey, however, continued to produce unusual designs, such as his Lite-line (from 1958). This was shaped like a rectangular box and had pre-formed aluminium sides, but it didn't catch on. Alper's Sprites, on the other hand, were successful as ever: new models, including the Alpine and Musketeer, sold in big numbers from 1958.

The 1950s witnessed the establishment of numerous other manufacturers, including Normandie, Penguin, Rodway, Scott Roadcraft, Balmforth, Carahomes, Knowsley, Marston, Bessacarr and Valley.

The unusual Coventry Steel Lite-line model in 1958 cost £563. Dawtrey, its designer and owner, tragically died in this year – a great loss to the caravan industry.

Explorer 14

Explorer 14 looking forward

Explorer 14 looking to the rear

FORWARD DESIGN AND LARGE CONCERNS: 1960–80

THE 1950S HAD seen some weird and wonderful designs, some of which worked while others were doomed to failure. In the 1960s and 1970s, the use of GRP increased; insulation improved and glass fibre and polystyrene were used in the roof and sides. Some makers such as Elddis in the 1960s would use tin foil for insulation, while Thomson used mineral wool. Chassis design had also improved, including a new system pioneered by B&B Trailers (who dominated the touring caravan chassis market) known as the Sigma auto reverse system. This meant the driver now didn't need to reset a reverse catch as was required on the older coupling designs.

All touring caravans by 1972 (apart from most specialist luxury makers such as Carlight, Safari, Stirling and Castleton) would fit pre-painted oven-baked aluminium exterior panels, which gave a long-lasting finish. Front drawbar-mounted gas bottle lockers would be common from 1973 (these were made of GRP) while real wood veneers on medium-priced tourers gave way to new stain-resistant photo veneered finishes.

Gas lighting would be replaced with interior 12-volt lights, while fridges, heaters and ovens were being fitted as standard on more expensive caravans. Glass windows, which were heavy, could break easily and caused condensation, were being slowly phased out with plastic units taking their place. On some luxury makes at the end of the 1970s, mains electrics were added in readiness for electric hook-up points on the ever-improving caravan sites.

Opposite: Explorer 14 (1972), from luxury makers Cheltenham Caravans, was launched to appeal to mid-market buyers and keep Cheltenham going through troubled times. The Explorer brand was dropped in 1974.

The speed limit for towing was raised in the 1960s from 30 mph to 40 mph and by 1973 increased to 50 mph. Caravan road rallying helped develop chassis design: longer drawbars and wider tracks were introduced, improving overall towing stability. Apart from the GRP panels being used in construction by luxury makes, a few manufacturers used special presses to glue the exterior aluminium to the polystyrene core insulation and framing, along with the interior wall board, pressing them together. This was used for the sides and by the mid-1980s it became a common method of constructing most touring caravans. It was known as 'bonded sandwich' construction.

This system was strong and light but expensive to produce. By the early 1970s Dormobile, Monolite and Sinclair Gordon had begun to use this method along with imported makes such as the Swedish maker Cabby, who used polyurethane as the wall core instead of polystyrene. By the mid-1970s most up-market caravan floors were insulated and used a sandwich construction with Styrofoam as its core.

The Ci group, formed in 1963 by the merger of Sprite, Eccles and Bluebird implemented a new construction

Sandwich construction was being looked at seriously in the early 1970s. Small Sunderland luxury maker Sinclair Gordon used this construction in 1971 – the van was so strong that several men could sit on the roof without damaging it.

system for 1975. This involved injecting Styrofoam into the walls of its Europa range of tourers. This proved expensive but was successful and by 1976 this method was used in the revised Eccles tourer range. It cost Ci over £2 million to prepare for the new construction method, and was used only in Eccles models and in the Europa range. The foam had excellent insulating qualities and gave a stronger body shell in the process.

The 1960s was a decade in which the luxury clubman touring caravan was in high demand. One maker, Stirling, had built up a good reputation from the 1950s building quality luxury hand-crafted tourers with a lantern roof. In 1960 it took on the Winchester name after Hutchings folded in 1959. Carlight was another luxury manufacturer; established in 1932, the name was held in high esteem by

Ribbed pannelling conceals new sealed foam sandwich construction for improved rigidity and insulation.

Ci used its new foam-injected construction in its Europa range (pictured) from 1974, first adopting it for the Eccles range from 1976. The changeover cost over £2 million, denting Ci's profits.

many caravanners who aspired to this luxury hand-built range (with a price tag of £900 back in 1963!).

In the early 1960s even more caravan-manufacturing concerns were added to the UK industry, again based in or near Hull, including Buccaneer, Ace, Swift, Mardon, Silverline, Embassy, Alpine Coachcraft (A-Line), Sovereign, Riviera, Minster, Volnay, Aaro, Haltemprice, Sabre, Eton and Royden. With access to easier exports, scenes at the Hull docks were often dominated by rows of caravans ready to be shipped abroad.

Most of the UK manufacturers exported heavily into Europe and beyond. To continental buyers, UK tourers were seen as stylish and well finished for their price. Hull maker, Ace Caravans (founded in 1962 by ex-Astral employee Terry Reed) exported most of its production output by 1963, and by the late 1960s had carved a large slice of the UK market with its medium-priced, well-designed tourers. Ace was innovative in being the first maker of mass-produced UK touring caravans to use GRP moulded exterior front and rear panels for its range in 1969.

Using moulded full-height end panels, the 1969 Aces were distinctive and stylish. But problems with the moulds – especially where the GRP joined the aluminium roof

Royden was a short-lived manufacturer from 1969, one of many companies that failed after just a couple of years. Royden caravans, built in Hull, were attractive clubman tourers and came with a high specification.

panel – caused leaks, so for 1970 Ace reverted to using traditional aluminium front and rear panels. Alpine Coachcraft (who later changed their name to A-Line Caravans) was founded in 1964 and by the late 1960s had begun to carve out a place in the mid-market sector, competing head on with Ace, Mardon and Swift. A-Line became known for its range of tourers named Super, as well as holiday homes and towable static holiday caravans. By the mid-1970s A-Line were producing motorhomes following their success in export markets.

Ace Caravans grew rapidly in the 1960s, and by 1969 had formed Ace Plastics, which built the front and rear panels for that year's Aces. Ace was the first mass-produced tourer to use front and rear moulded panels.

In 1964, Hull-based Ken Smith started building a range of mid-priced tourers, called Swift. By the late 1960s the range had gained a good reputation, offering quality interiors and distinctive design. One of their features was a cool store built into the floor and excellent through-vision from the tow car. By the mid-1970s Swift had firmly established itself, though sadly Ken Smith died suddenly in late 1972. His wife Joan and son Peter carried on the business, developing it over the subsequent decades.

Lesley Marshall, together with his wife, founded Mardon caravans in 1963 (having previously worked for Willerby), making small, lightweight caravans. Distinctive features included stainless steel front stone guards and padded vinyl interior wall finishes.

Astral caravans, established in 1959, were part of a large timber-importing family business (Spooner Group) that soon grew to be the largest caravan manufacturer by the late 1960s in Hull. The Spooner family caravanned using their Astral caravans and often implemented new models and layouts following

their own touring experiences. One model developed through this experience was the Astral Sunrise. It had a Luton top (protruding over the drawbar), which housed a bed. Bluebird produced an almost identical design in 1963, a year before Astral, named the Joie de Vivre (also priced around £390). But sales proved disappointing and both manufacturers' versions were dropped.

By 1970 Astral was the largest manufacturer of tourers in Hull, with vast export markets. The pictures on page 40 illustrate the Ranger, mainly for UK buyers; below is the export equivalent, named Apollo.

Bill Knott's Bluebird Company had evolved into a massive concern by the early 1960s. Sprite, which in 1960 had acquired Eccles Caravans, moved Eccles production from Birmingham to Sprite's Newmarket headquarters. Sprite had expanded fast with rising sales, and both had grown such that in order to expand further more resources and finances would be needed. In July 1963, after months of rumours, Sprite/Eccles joined Bluebird, forming a new company, Caravans International, better known as the Ci Group.

Sam Alper became Chairman of the new Ci Group, and Knott left after just a few years, eventually founding BK Holiday Caravans.

The new Ci commanded greater buying power from suppliers; this in turn meant that prices could be kept low while new designs and development were worked on across the ranges. Before long, Ci had acquired German maker Wilk Caravans in 1964/5, causing a certain amount of alarm among other German caravan manufacturers at the time.

Ci next acquired Welsh manufacturer Fairholme Products. Under founder/owner Jim Hennessey, Fairholme had grown in the 1950s to become a well-respected make of high-quality yet affordable touring caravans. Fairholme became the luxury arm of the Ci Group.

As Eccles production was moved to Newmarket, so Fairholme followed in 1969. Bluebird's Europe tourer range was transferred to the Newmarket plant from the Parkstone factory in Dorset at around the same time. The Europe name was dropped in 1970 and re-launched as Europa for 1971, with new-look continental styling, enforcing the Ci Group's influence in design and style.

Ci would expand further, taking in more manufacturers as far afield as South Africa and New Zealand. Danish awning manufacturer OBI became part of Ci, along with several other companies connected with supplying caravan components and accessories. Sprites had become top sellers in Europe; with such extensive testing, dedicated design teams and huge development budgets, the Sprite caravan was untouchable by its competitors (at least until the mid-1970s).

A further increase in new concerns – manufacturers such as Gold Star, Avon, Elddis, Dalesman, Estuary, Colonial, Fleetwood, Regency, Fleetwind, Olympic, Shult, Viking, SBQ, Albatross and Abbey – continued to occur in the 1960s. Some of these went out of business months after starting up, while others lasted just a few years longer. With sales prone to highs and lows, the caravan industry could prove volatile. After the Second World War, Bailey and Sprite witnessed the 1960s as a time of great expansion. Bailey's sales increased at home and in the rest of Europe; by this period the company had developed a familiar body profile that buyers recognised, being tweaked through to the early 1980s.

Elddis Caravans, established in 1964 by Siddle Cook and his son Raymond, had just one model. Five years later this model had six layouts, two version of each being named after winds – Whirlwind, Tornado and Cyclone. They left Elddis in 1978 to set up Compass Caravans, not far from

Established in 1964, by 1971 the Elddis profile had fully emerged. The 1971 Cyclone pictured was the company's largest tourer; by 1973 Elddis had been bought out by ABI Caravans.

Dormobile planned to be one of the biggest touring caravan manufacturers by 1971/2, but as they discovered, a new factory and machinery didn't necessarily sell caravans. Pictured is the 3.2 family model from 1970.

the Elddis works in County Durham. (Ironically it would be Elddis who took over the Compass name in the 1990s.)

Motorhome manufacturer Dormobile joined the booming touring caravan market in September 1969. With a factory dedicated to tourers, its low-priced three-model range had sandwich sides made by special presses in the factory. Dormobile also spray-painted their tourers, when most manufacturers bought in pre-painted aluminium.

Plans to produce four thousand caravans a year and be the UK's third biggest manufacturer by the early 1970s never materialised. Dormobile in 1971/2 decided to change its market sector and launched a luxury model named the Kent, but sales were limited and production stopped. It was not until 1977 that Dormobile would re-enter the tourer market, with greater success. The Dormobile body was glued onto the chassis/floor – an unusual form of construction – while the sides and ends were bonded one-piece panels, as used on most modern tourers today. The Dormobile range proved a success but production stopped in 1980 with Dormobile motorhomes going into liquidation.

Thomson, the well-established Scottish manufacturer, had by the mid-1960s grown into a major player with their mid-priced quality tourers benefiting from a distinctive style and a good range of layouts. At one stage Thomson had a factory in Belgium and bought land to develop caravan parks, along with a purpose-built showroom in Glasgow. Names such as Glendale, Mini-Glen and Glenelg were top-selling models in the Thomson line-up.

Another successful tourer range that appeared in 1966 was built by Estuary Caravans, branded as Cavalier. These tourers were again mid-priced and had a virtual box profile being relieved with curved corners, top and bottom. Roy Cattell (ex-Nene Valley Caravans) had developed the new vans and it wasn't long before the Felixstowe factory was expanding.

By the end of the 1960s Thomson was the second largest tourer manufacturer in the UK. The Glenmore (left) and Gleneagle (right) were large family models produced in 1969. Thomson was the last large producer to spray its own exterior panels, continuing until 1971.

The simple profile of the Estuary (Cavalier) gave excellent interior space; the 1000T shown here (1970) slept four, had a loo compartment and could be towed by cars such as the BMC Austin/Morris 1100.

Lightweight and with spacious interiors, the Cavalier also built up large export markets. Cavalier layouts featured L-shaped lounges and kitchens. By 1970 Cattell had left Cavalier to start up mid-priced Panther Caravans, which proved another successful tourer range in the 1970s.

Chandlery makers Cosalt in Grimsby had diversified into caravans in 1966 under the name Humber Caravans, with Abbey as its brand of tourers. As was usual in that period, exports played a major part in their progress. Abbey would soon begin to compete strongly with Swift and Elddis in the UK. Cosalt bought out luxury maker Safari Caravans in 1968, and in 1973 acquired Riviera Caravans, strengthening the company as a major manufacturer.

Regency, a luxury maker founded in 1964 in Birkenhead, constructed its luxury tourers with GRP for the sides, ends and roof of its tourers – an advanced idea of caravan manufacture that was unusual at the time. Sandwich-constructed floors were also introduced, using injected polyurethane foam between two sections of marine ply. Regency's other notable features included the high specification: hot water, fridge, oven, electric brakes and torsion bar suspension, shower, flued gas heater and 12-volt lighting. Regency had a distinctive profile, but was not the most attractive tourer range to look at; they proved surprisingly popular for a few years, but the firm had gone out of production by late 1970, producing an outstanding list of fourteen models for the 1969 model year.

By 1970 the touring caravan-buying boom was in full swing and other manufacturers joined the ever-growing

Cosalt set up Humber Caravans in 1966 after building insulated containers for Ross Fish Products. Branded the Abbey, the 12 model shown here was produced from 1966.

Regency Cruisers used GRP panels for all its construction. This is the 1968 export model, based on the Gem. Looks were not Regency's strong point but at least this range was distinctive.

market. In the Hull area names such as Beverley Coachcraft, Churchill, Trinity, Elite, Apollo, Trio, Tranby, Eagle and Castle were all new. Other makes such as Trophy, Panther, Reed, Cosy Car, Chad, Avondale, Lunar, Victor, Ski, Compass, FC, Forrest, Carapace, Dormobile, Cotswold, Mustang, Monolite, Viscount and Boomerang were more new names setting up in this period. The demand couldn't sustain such a crowded market, however; in April 1973 VAT was added to touring caravans, pushing prices up considerably. The economic slowdown and petrol/oil shortages by 1974 damaged sales further. Most of the names mentioned above would fall victim to the downturn.

In 1972 Ace Caravans merged with its neighbour Belmont, makers of holiday homes, to form Ace Belmont International or ABI. This merger now rivalled Ci and gave this new concern extra buying power as well as increasing its ranges to include Monza, Target and Award. ABI would further strengthen its position buying out the popular Elddis brand in 1973.

Ci from 1973 had instigated Ci solus dealerships to force competitors off the forecourt. The idea wasn't popular among all dealers. The Gailey Group, a large dealership, dropped Ci and took on more of ABI's ranges, but most dealers did go over to Ci who were able to support them with sales promotions and dedicated spares back-up and sales training schemes.

Touring caravan sales by the end of the 1970s had shrunk

By 1975 Swift was one of the smartest-looking mid-priced tourers on the market. Quality interiors and excellent towing stability saw Swift increase its market share.

to 44,000 units a year (from over 80,000 in 1973). Even respected manufacturers such as Knowsley (1976) would fall by the wayside, although Knowsley was relaunched by Wigan-based Pemberton holiday homes after they bought the name. Cheltenham had launched its Explorer mid-priced range in 1972 to try to capture more sales, but by 1975 had ceased production. After a stalled re-start under the name Stirling Caravans, Cheltenham resurfaced as Ferndown in 1978.

Manchester-based Lynton Caravans had one-time Ci designer Reg Dean employed as Head of Marketing and Design. Dean's classic, clean lines and very modern domestic-influenced interiors gave Lynton an identity as well as increased sales from 1967. Some years later Dean moved to ABI, designing the new modern-looking Target range in 1975 before moving to A-Line Caravans in 1976. Dean revamped their tourers with the Crown and Rambler

Ci used Tom Karren from Ogle Design in an effort to make its tourers more eye-catching and harder to copy. This is the Fairholme 425, one of Karren's designs from 1970.

By 1973, ABI had become second in size to Ci, helped by the launch of its Monza range, which was better finished than the Sprite yet cost little more. ABI would become the UK's foremost tourer manufacture by 1982.

ranges and a lightweight budget model named the Imp – a three-berth, 3-metre-long caravan.

Ci had developed its touring ranges with vast financial investment; the Eccles range benefited from this, using industrial designer Tom Karren, who added plastic body mouldings onto the Eccles Amethyst for 1970 along with Fairholme's 425 model. Eccles proved the success story; the 425 only achieved moderate sales. Sprite sales were hit by the entry-level Monza range from ABI (launched in 1973), with which it competed head-on.

Imported makes were thin on the ground in the 1960s with attempts by Tabbert, Constructram, and Caravelair

failing to lure UK buyers. By the next decade, however, imports began to make some inroads into the UK market. Yugoslavian maker Adria hit UK shores in 1970 after gaining market share in Europe in just over five years. Adria would become the most successful imported tourer in the UK, succeeding where most imports faltered.

Adria proved to be successful when it entered the UK market in 1970, providing buyers with an alternative touring caravan design. They were well equipped, but cost more than equivalent UK models.

A NEW ERA: THE 1980s TO THE PRESENT

THE START OF the 1980s saw caravan sales slumping to 22,000 units, sending most manufacturers out of business. Dealerships suffered too: even the large Gailey Group closed eventually. Astral, once the biggest manufacturer in the Hull area, closed its doors in March 1980. They had been one of the first UK major manufacturers to use the German brand Al-Ko chassis in 1977 with its Shadow range. Al-Ko dominated the UK touring caravan chassis market by 1982 after buying out B&B Trailers.

By 1985, Stirling, Royale, Cheltenham, Mustang, Churchill, Welton, A-Line (Deanline), Viking, Cavalier, Dormobile, Thomson, Comanche, Robin, Cougar and Elite had all closed. Even industry giant, Caravans International, became a victim of the downturn at the end of 1982; Sam Alper was forced to walk away, leaving the brands and factories to be sold off.

By early 1983 a new Ci at Newmarket was born, smaller and more efficient, and producing Sprite, Eccles, Elite and Europa ranges once again. The new company was quick to design and develop new models and within a few years new ranges such as Cosmos and Esprit were launched.

ABI had seen sales tumble; they turned their attention to new designs, producing lighter, more affordable, better-equipped and styled models. In 1981 ABI launched its limited edition super-aerodynamic Typhoon (£5,975) two-model range. Integral front gas locker and new bonded sandwich construction (a polystyrene core bonded to

Opposite: Silverline had re-emerged in 1984 with the niche Nova micro touring caravan. From 1989, the Silverline Nova Princess was selling well, but by 1993 the company had gone out of business.

The ABI Typhoon from 1982 proved touring caravan design could be exciting. The new limited edition Typhoons gave way to the ABI luxury Award from 1983.

board on the interior and aluminium on the exterior) saved weight while interiors were kept traditional yet modern.

ABI designers had cleverly integrated the traditional front chest of drawers in the lounge area into the nose of the Typhoon. This resulted in increased lounge space proving a sales success. A design classic, it took the Earls Court Caravan Show by storm in November 1981. The Typhoon profile was used for ABI's up-market Award range for 1983. It was a gamble but it paid off and by the end of the 1983 season the Awards had become top sellers for ABI.

Hull maker A-Line, once a large concern, had hit financial problems in the early 1980s. It was unable to

Avondale originated in 1970, and by the 1990s its Clubman range had developed as among the most pleasing and aerodynamic touring caravans on the market. The Sandmartin from 1991 was an end-kitchen two-berth model.

recover its original market share and in June 1981 the company went out of business. Designer Reg Dean bought the company and machinery, and within a few months was trading as Deanline Caravans. In February 1985, ABI purchased Deanline; two of the ranges from the old Deanline Company, Crown and Golden Crown, were produced in 1986 at the Elddis factory; the Crowns lasted just one model year only.

Luxury maker Avondale, founded in 1970 by Gerald Ball, produced distinctive, lightweight tourers. Avondale soon had a loyal customer base, and by the mid-1970s the company was also producing a range of entry-level tourers named Perle. By 1979 Avondale launched into the mid-price market with its Leda range. The company would see considerable growth from 1985 and at one point they branched out into caravan park ownership. With strong exports and some eye-catching profiles, Avondale became a major player, but only until 2008, when poor sales led to its demise.

Preston-based Lunar Caravans had built up a reputation for high-quality lightweight tourers starting from humble

By the mid-1970s Lunar had quickly established itself in a crowded marketplace. By 1975 it had entered the upper luxury market with the Clubman range.

beginnings in an old barn near Wigan in Lancashire. Lunar's founders, Brian Talbot and Ken Wilcox, were employed by Knowsley Caravans before setting up Lunar in July 1969. By the early 1980s Lunar were building their own aluminium chassis (TW Chassis) and also manufacturing their own GRP moulded panels for their new exterior designs. Lunar developed its show-stoppers, the Clubman and Deltas for 1985, which had wrap-around GRP front panel and full-moulded GRP roof sections. Bonded construction and an aluminium chassis kept weight down; lightweight furniture fittings were also used.

The demise of caravan manufacturing at the beginning of the decade saw the sudden sales upturn in 1985 take those left by surprise, with production falling short of demand. This mini boom in caravan sales in the mid-1980s witnessed the start-up of several new caravan manufacturing concerns, including Vanroyce, Coachman, Andromeda, Centaur and – after a few years' absence in tourers – Silverline. Out of these new names Vanroyce and Coachman became quickly established. Vanroyce produced luxury, competitively priced tourers, using a GRP roof and front and rear panels. Vanroyce would eventually be bought out by ABI in the early 1990s. Elddis parted company with ABI in 1990 to become part of the Constantine Group in 1994.

Coachman, which was formed by ex-ABI employees George Kemp and Jim Hibbs in Hull from September 1986, concentrated on mid-priced, well-equipped tourers. Within a few years they had expanded their line-up to include the luxury VIP and entry-level Mirage ranges. By 1997 they were under the Explorer Group (the parent company to Elddis). Compass and luxury maker Buccaneer would also become part of Elddis.

Swift Caravans had increased its market share, remaining traditional in design and build since the 1970s and early 1980s. By the mid-1980s they were taking aerodynamic design more seriously with wind tunnel testing. This would lead to the introduction of its Cottingham range in 1981, complete with raked front and rear back panel including a moulded roof spoiler. The Challenger range in 1985 superseded the Cottingham using a GRP front panel and GRP rear roof spoiler. The Challenger was well equipped and would influence the luxury Swift Corniche range in using GRP for improved aerodynamics. The 1989 Swift Corniche was announced as the Wind of Change in caravan design with up-to-the-minute styling with the extensive use of GRP.

With GRP becoming easier to use and lower in price, many entry-level models used the material by the late 1980s. Ci also developed new, aerodynamic tourers with their Cosmos and Elite ranges, which relied heavily on moulded plastics, complemented by modern interiors.

Silverline Caravans at York re-emerged as a tourer manufacturer in 1984 after hitting hard times at the end of the 1970s. With the upturn, Silverline went into the micro-caravan market with its Nova range. Two-berth lightweight narrow-bodied tourers were stylish, carving out a niche market. This era was no doubt about style and lightweight materials. It was also the period when designers

The year 1989 saw the new generation of Corniche launched by Swift; extensive use of GRP mouldings gave the exterior good aerodynamics and distinctive looks.

were encouraged to produce some startling interiors, as we shall see.

Cosalt's Abbey launched its SR range in 1985, equipped with sports wheels, red flash striping, interiors with red sinks, hobs and space heaters, and grey- and red-striped upholstery. ABI with the Monza-based Mode range (1987) featured red and grey furniture; Avondale, similarly, used grey and yellow interiors on their Mayfair range. Ci went down this route with its 1987 Sprite Finesse range, and Coachman's Concept range in 1996 boasted grey-based interiors, but the market was limited and by 1989 the trendy look had gone.

The 1980s had produced some advanced profiles using plastics and GRP mouldings, helped by computer-aided design, which drove touring caravan evolution. One advanced design was the Ci Voyager, launched in 1988. It had extensive plastic mouldings for the front and rear panels. The interior incorporated ash-finished furniture with aircraft-styled lockers and blue soft furnishings. There were twin opening sun roofs, a full oven, Alde wet central heating, fridge, auto-operated jockey wheel and corner steadies, microwave, on-board battery, roof-mounted solar panel, full mains, hot water, shower, cassette loo and an on-board water tank. Way ahead of its time and expensive, few were sold; years later it was built in Australia, manufactured by Road Star Caravans.

In the late 1980s many touring caravans featured more equipment as standard, such as flyscreens and blinds, heaters, electrics, fridges, mains lighting, double-glazing, showers and hot water. In 1987 Thetford launched its cassette loo for touring caravans; it was hygienic and easy to empty.

In the early 1990s new sales slowed down. Several manufacturers such as Mardon, Silverline and Ci finished; Ci would re-emerge as Sprite Leisure Ltd. Sprite Leisure introduced new innovations to its ranges such as loose-fit carpets, halogen lighting and gas barbecue points and exterior shower connections. Sprite Leisure was acquired by Swift in late 1993; now renamed Sterling, production moved up to Swift's Cottingham plant. Swift had also acquired luxury maker Cotswold Coachcraft in 1989, well known for its classic-looking Windrush models. Cosalt (owners of Abbey), which included Welton and Safari, closed its Grimsby factory, selling the names to Swift in 1992.

ABI was reputed to have fields of unsold models in 1997. By 1998 when ABI collapsed, the company was saved and re-named ABI UK under its new owners. By April 2001, tourer production had been halted to concentrate on the holiday home market. Its rival, Swift, bought all the ABI tourer names such as Ace, Jubilee and Award, re-launching them under the Swift Group.

In 1996 Bailey staged an aggressive stance with its Ranger series. Low weights and prices (below £10,000) with good layout choices, plus a specification to match more expensive models, the Rangers became bestsellers. Before long Bailey had increased sales of its Senators and Pageants, offering more value than its competitors. In 2005 Bailey had overtaken Elddis, Lunar and Avondale in sales and was seriously attacking Swift's market share.

Excellent value and sharp marketing gave Bailey an edge that was hard to beat. Swift re-launched Sprite onto the UK market in 2005 to compete directly with the Ranger, which within a few years had become well established. Bailey could adapt and upgraded its Rangers quickly to keep up with contemporary trends. Elddis developed new models such as its Genesis range, with its futuristic profile and almost Art Deco design interior.

The new millennium witnessed increased tourer sales, with Swift and Bailey firmly leading the competition. Suffolk-based Fleetwood Caravans had been successful with its medium-priced Colchester range from the late

Elddis launched the Genesis in 1996. It sold in limited numbers but its design influenced other Elddis ranges from 1998.

1960s. By the 1980s they were producing entry models such as the Garland range and entered the luxury sector with its Heritage range in 1999. Heritage models had some excellent layouts including the ever-popular fixed bed configuration. Fleetwood was the first UK maker to fit the large Heki roof vents and fit the Alde wet central heating system to a full range of tourers.

Although some manufacturers had ceased, several small concerns were established, including Stealth Caravans, although this company had limited success with their 'dare to be different' exteriors and contemporary interior design. Eterniti also joined the touring caravan's ranks with its side-extending tourers, while Welsh manufacturer Fifth Wheel Caravans launched two luxury tourers with extending sides.

Children's bunks became popular for most family models. Microwaves and TV aerials were standard, along with blown air heating and fitted radios. Caravan construction, however, had remained virtually the same since the early 1980s, until Bailey in 2010 launched their new Pegasus range using their Alu-Tech branded construction. Using plastic composite framing (replacing timber) and dispensing with front and rear moulded

The 2010 Stealth Intrepid was a creation of Dunster House, sold direct to the public. The front GRP nose moulded panel could be ordered in different colours.

panels, producing them was faster and cheaper. Bailey dropped its long-standing ranges, replacing them with new Alu-Tech ranges.

Swift in 2011 launched its new industry-leading aerodynamic profiles with integrated sunroof in the front roof panel. The new look moved touring caravan styling on, influencing other manufacturers' designs in the process. In 2014 the company launched its new construction method (Smart) with polyurethane for its framework, replacing wood. In Elddis' latest models, walls and floors are bonded

Bailey launched its controversial Pegasus range for 2010, with a more minimalist interior compared with the Senator it had replaced. Alu-Tech was Bailey's construction system, which limited profile design.

The 2014 Eccles interior is contemporary and shows how modern tourers have advanced since those early days.

(Solid), and Lunar uses a new lightweight honeycomb wall board (Core), lowering the weight further.

With new innovations in styling and construction, touring caravans provide all the comforts of home yet offer the sense of freedom that no other holiday can provide. From the first Eccles trailer caravan in 1919, the Rileys could surely never have dreamt of the touring caravan's enduring popularity, nearly a hundred years on.

Lunar's new look for 2013 was used on Lexon, Clubman and Delta ranges, but they refrained from adding a sunroof.

FURTHER READING

Ellesmore, Roger. *British Caravans Before World War II*. Herridge & Sons, 2012.

First in the Field. various authors, Camping & Caravanning Club, 2001.

Jenkinson, Andrew. *Caravans 1919–1959*. Veloce Publishing, 1997.

Jenkinson, Andrew. *Caravans 1960–2001*. Veloce Publishing, 1999.

Jenkinson, Andrew. *The Story of Sprite Caravans*. Veloce Publishing, 2011.

Smith, Len. *A Caravan Holiday in 1932*. Forgotten Titles, 2009.

Whiteman, Bill. *History of the Caravan*. Blandford Press, 1973.

PLACES TO VISIT

Beaulieu Motor Museum, Brokenhurst, Hampshire, SO42 7ZN. Telephone: 01590 612345.
Website: www.beaulieu.co.uk

Cotswold Motor Museum, The Old Mill, Sherborne Street, Bourton-on-the-Water, Gloucestershire GL54 2BY. Telephone: 01451 821255.
Website: www.cotswoldmotoringmuseum.co.uk

Gaydon Motor Heritage Centre, Banbury Road, Gaydon, Warwickshire CV35 0BJ. Telephone: 01926 641188.
Website: www.heritage-motor-centre.co.uk

Lakeland Motor Museum, Old Blue Mill, Backbarrow, Ulverston LA12 8TA. Telephone: 015395 30400.
Website: www.lakelandmotormuseum.co.uk

INDEX

References to images are in *italic*.

A-Line Caravans 49–50, 53, 54–5
Abbey 42, 46, *47*, 58
Ace Belmont International (ABI) 48, 49, 50, *50*, 53–4, 55, 56, 58, 59
Ace Caravans 21, 22–3, *23*, 38–9, *39*, 48
Adria 51, *51*
Aerodynamics 15, 17, 19
Airlite Caravans 21–2, *22*
Alcock, Frederick 6
Alper, Sam 28, 29, 41, 53
Alpine range *24*, 33
Alpine Coachcraft 38, 39; *see also* A-Line Caravans
Aluminium 31, 32, 35, 36, 38–9, 56
Amphibian designs 33
Angela 10–11
Apollo range *41*
Astral 32, 40–1, *41*, 53
Avondale 48, *54*, 55, 58, 59
Award range 48, 54, 59
Bailey 26, 32, *32*, 42–3, 59, 60–1
Bakelite 22
Ball, Gerald 55
Ball coupling 20, *20*
Bathrooms 19, 47, 58, 59
B&B Trailers 31, 35, 53
Beds 41, 60
Berkeley Caravans 26, 29–30, *30*, 33
Bessacar 28, 33
Bluebird 26–7, *27*, 36, 41, 42
Bristol Coach & Wagon Company 5
Buccaneer 29, 38, 56
Car Cruiser 7, 14, 17–18, *18*, 25
Caravan Club 5–6, 7, 13, 25
Carlight 14, 21, 35, 37–8
Cars 6–7, 9, 11, 15, 25, 32
Cattell, Roy 45, 46
Cavalier range 45–6, *46*, 53
Chassis 8, 16, 19–20, 31, 35, 36, 53, 56
Cheltenham 9, 14, 17, *17*, 19–20, 31, *31*, *34*, 49, 53
Churchill 48, 53
Ci (Caravans International) Group 36–7, *37*, 41, 42, 48, *49*, 50, 53, 57, 58
Cliffe 7, *7*
Clubman range *54*, *55*, 56
Coachman 56, 58
Colchester range 59–60
Compass Caravans 43–4, 48, 56
Concept range 58
Cook, Siddle 43
Cooking facilities 8, 11, 31, 35, 47, 58
Corniche range 57, *57*
Coronation range 17, 31
Cosalt 46–7, 58, 59
Cosmos range 53, 57
Cotswold Coachcraft 21, 48, 59
Cottingham range 57
Courier range *30*
Coventry Steel Caravans 21, 22, *23*, 33
Cox, Wilkinson 8–9
Crown range 49, 55
Cyclone range 43, *43*

Dawtrey, Clifford 21, 22, 25, 33
Dealerships 21, 48, 53
Dean, Reg 49–50, 55
Design development 20, 58
Dormobile 36, 44, *44*, 48, 53
Eccles Transport Company 7, *7*, 8, 10, *10*, 11, *11*, 13, 14–16, *16*, 17, 25, 26, 31, 36, 37, 41, 42, 62, *62*
Elddis 35, 42, 43, *43*, 46, 48, 56, 59, 61–2
Electricity 35, 58, 59
Elf range 28, *28*
Elite 48, 53, 57
Ensor, Charles 7, 11
Enterprise range 26, *26*
Estuary Caravans 42, 45–6
Europa range 29, 37, *37*, 42, 53
Europe 15, 16–17, 29, 38, 42
Explorer range *34*, 49, 56
Exports 15–17, 38, 46
Fairholme 425 *49*, 50
Family Four range 19, *19*
Flatvan 10
Fleetwood Caravans 42, 59–60
Folding caravans 10, 11
Furniture 15, 56, 58
Gailey Group 48, 53
Gardeners, the 9
Gas 14, 31, 35
Genesis range 59, *60*
Glass-reinforced plastic (GRP) 29–30, 31, *31*, 35, 36, 38–9, 47, 56, 57, 58
Glider *14*, 21
Hart, Melvin 10
Heating 31, 35, 47, 58, 60
Hennessey, Jim 42
Hibbs, Jim 56
Holder, George 29
Horses 6, 7, *9*
Hull 32, 38, 39, 48, 56
Hutchings, Bertram 9, 37
Insulation 20, 22, 29, 31, 35, 36
Interior design 22, 40, 49, 54, 58–9
Intrepid range *61*
Jubilee Caravans *12*, 21
Jubilee range 59
Junior Car Club 13
Karren, Tom 50
Kemp, George 56
Knott, Bill 26–7, 41–2
Knowsley Caravans 33, 49, 56
Lighting 8, 19, 31, 35, 47, 58, 59
Lite-line range 33, *33*
Lunar Caravans 48, 55–6, 59, *62*
Lynton Caravans 49
Maestro range 32, *32*
Mardon 38, 39, 40, 58
Marshall, Lesley 40
Minor range 27
Molly Croft roof design 9–10
Monolite 36, 48
Monza range 48, 50, *50*
Musketeer range *3*, 33
Mustang 48, 53
National Caravan Council 14

National range 17
Nomad Caravans 14
Nova range *52*, 57
Paladin Trailavan Company 26, 29
Panter, Charles 29–30
Panther Caravans 46, 48
Pathfinder range 27, *27*
Peak Caravans 31, 33
Pegasus range 60–1, *61*
Pemberton 26, 49
Phantom Knight range 22, *23*
Piggott 7, 10
Polystyrene 35, 36
President range 17
Rallies 13, 32
Rambler range 27, 49
Ranger range *40*, 59
Raven 7, 8–9, 14, 18–19, 25, 33
Regency 42, 47, *47*
Rice 11
Rileys 7–8, 14, 25
Riviera Caravans 38, 46
Robin range 30, 32, 53
Royden 38, *38*
Safari Caravans 26, 27–8, *28*, 35, 46, 59
Sandwich construction 36, *36*, 47, 53–4
Senator range 17, 59
Shadow range 11, 53
Siddall 19, *19*, 30–1
Silverline Caravans 38, *52*, 56, 57–8
Sinclair Gordon 36, *36*
Smith, Ken 39–40
Springbok range *31*
Sprite range *24*, 28–9, 33, 36, 41, 42, 43, 50, 53, 59
Sprite Leisure Ltd 58–9
Stables, Dr Gordon *4*, 5
Stealth Caravans 60, *61*
Stirling 35, 37, 53
Stone, J. Harris 6
Streamlining 15, 17, 18, 19
Streamlite 26, 28–9
Sunrise range 41
Swift Caravans 38, 39–40, 46, *48*, 56–7, 59, 61
Talbot, Brian 56
Target range 48, 49
Thomson 10, 25, 35, 45, *45*, 53
Toilets 11, 20–1, 58
Towing 8, 14, 20, 32, 36
Typhoon range 53–4, *54*
Universal range 30, *31*
Vanroyce 56
Viking 42, 53
Voyager range 58
Wanderer, The *4*, 5
Water 16, 19, 47, 58
Welton 32, 53, 59
Wilcox, Ken 56
Willerby Caravans 26, 30, *31*, 40
Williams, Fleming 'Streamline Bill' 17
Winchester 7, *8*, 9, 14, 19, 37
Windrush range 59
Wisdom range 29, *29*
Wizard range 18–19, *19*